Nina Simone
The Piano Songbook
Volume 2

© 2008 by Faber Music Ltd
First published by Faber Music Ltd in 2008
Bloomsbury House
74–77 Great Russell Street
London WC1B 3DA

Arranged by Chris Hussey
Engraved by Camden Music
Edited by Lucy Holliday

Designed by Lydia Merrills-Ashcroft
Cover photograph © Bob Willoughby/Redferns Music Picture Library

Printed in England by Caligraving Ltd
All rights reserved

ISBN10: 0-571-53035-4
EAN13: 978-0-571-53035-9

Reproducing this music in any form is illegal and
forbidden by the Copyright, Designs and Patents Act, 1988

To buy Faber Music publications or to find out about the full range of titles available,
please contact your local music retailer or Faber Music sales enquiries:

Faber Music Ltd, Burnt Mill, Elizabeth Way, Harlow, CM20 2HX England
Tel: +44(0)1279 82 89 82   Fax: +44(0)1279 82 89 83
sales@fabermusic.com   fabermusicstore.com

Angel Of The Morning 06

Baltimore 12

Black Is The Colour Of My True Love's Hair 19

Break Down And Let It All Out 22

I Get Along Without You Very Well 28

I Shall Be Released 34

I'm Gonna Leave You 40

Lilac Wine 46

My Man's Gone Now 50

New World Coming 56

The Pusher 66

Seems I'm Never Tired Lovin' You 75

Strange Fruit 84

Turn Me On 80

Wild Is The Wind 87

ANGEL OF THE MORNING

Words and Music by Chip Taylor

© 1967 EMI Blackwood Music Inc
EMI Songs Ltd

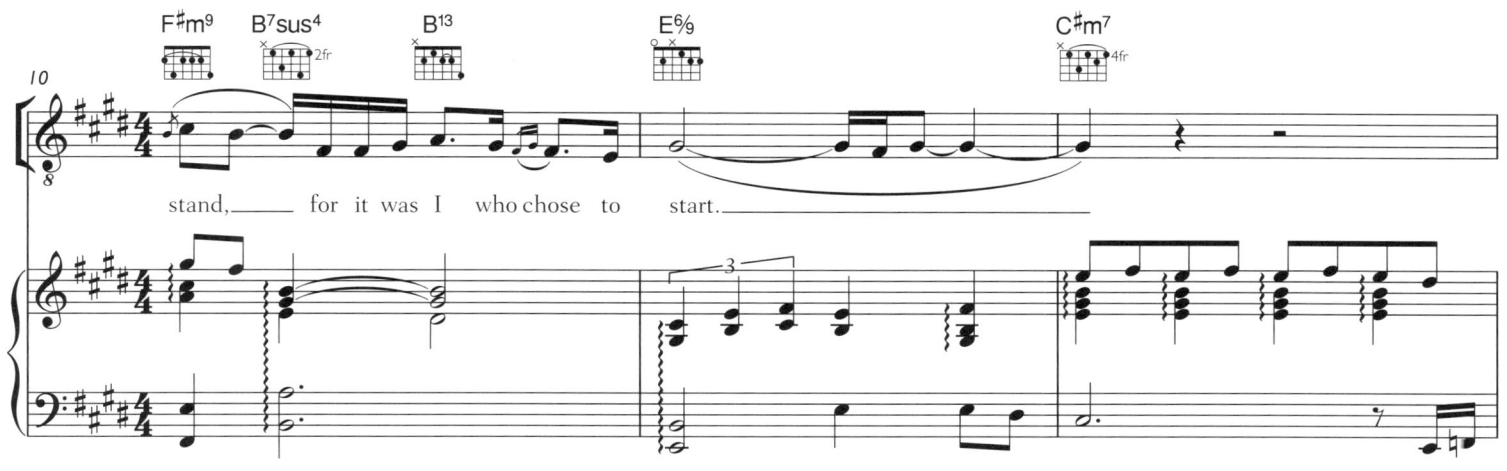

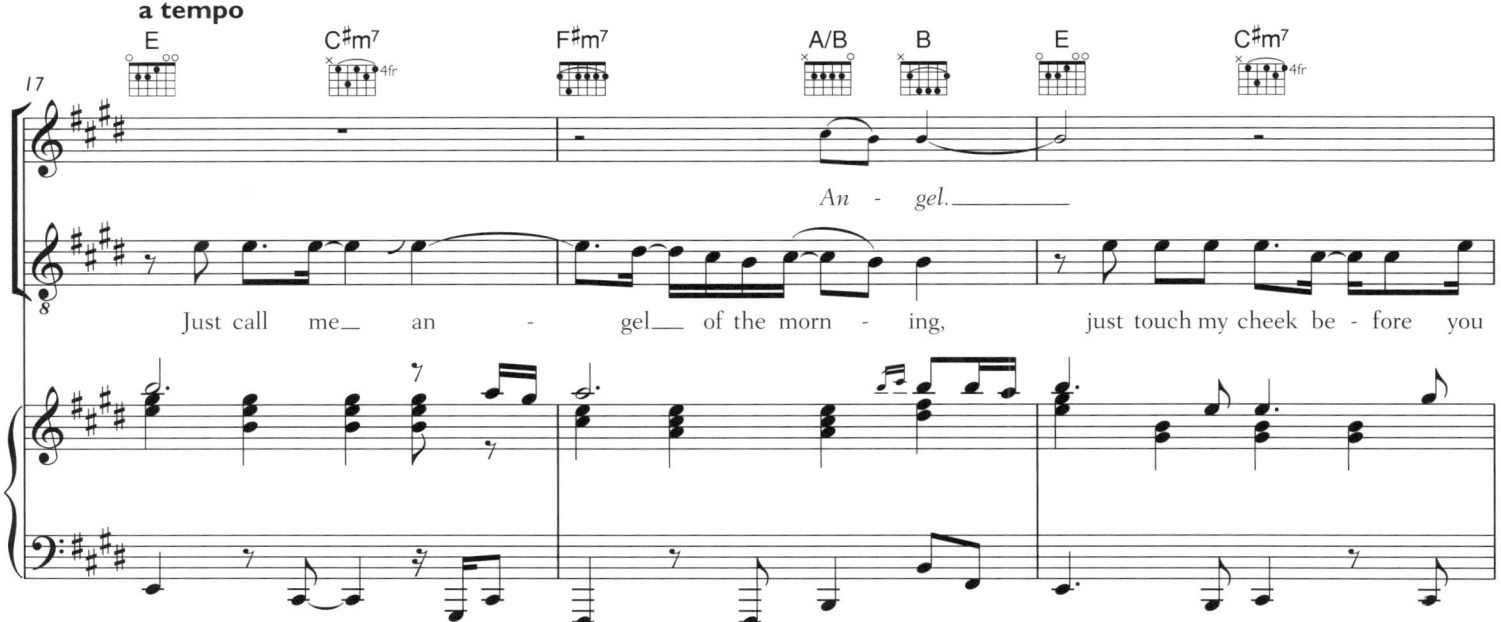

BALTIMORE

Words and Music by Randy Newman

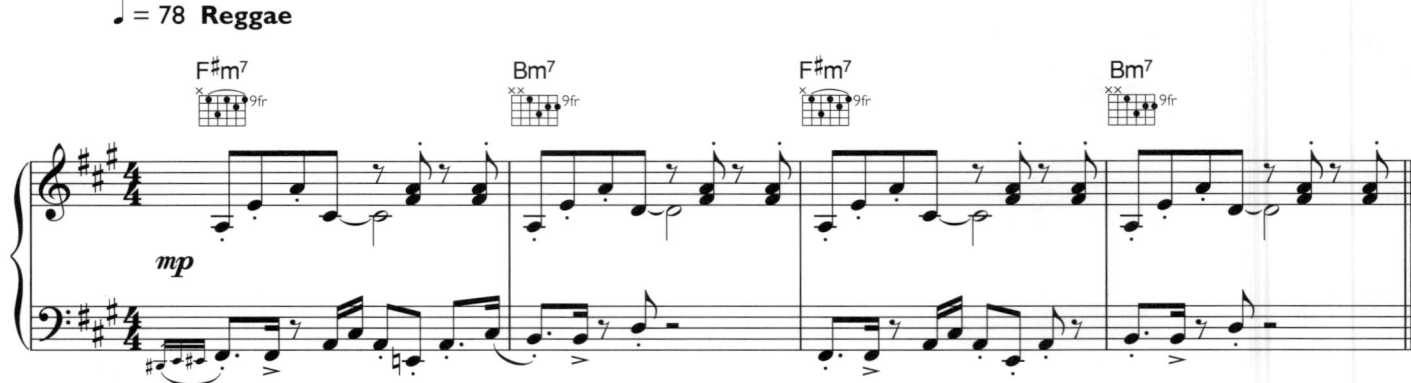

© 1977 Six Pictures Music
Warner/Chappell North America Ltd

BLACK IS THE COLOUR OF MY TRUE LOVE'S HAIR

Words and Music Traditional
Arranged by Nina Simone

Original key: A♭ minor

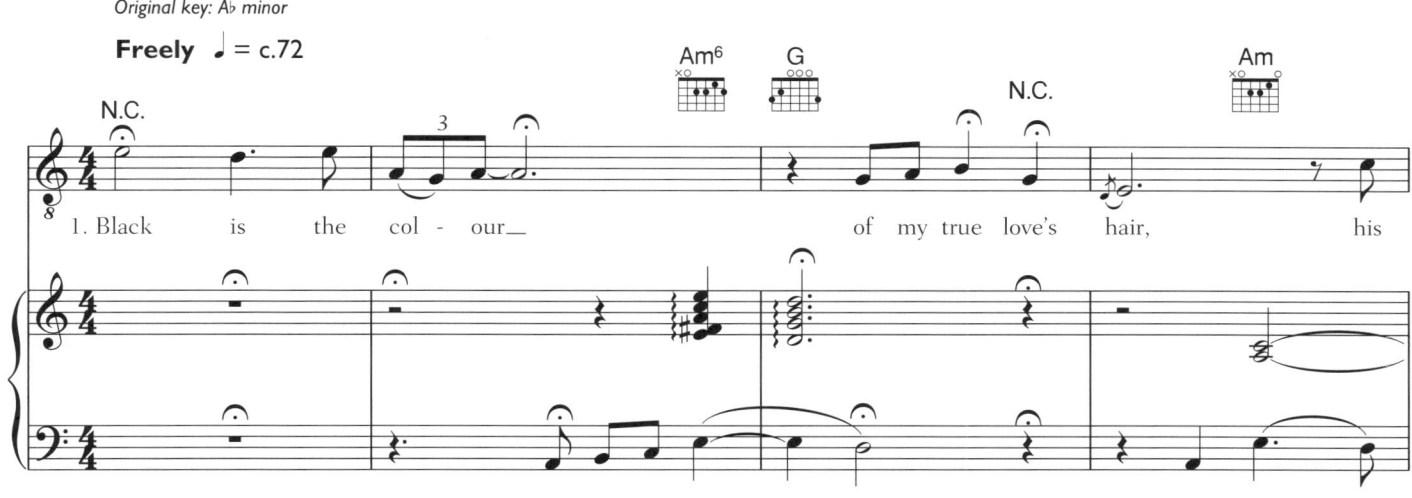

© 1959 Sam Fox Publishing Co Inc
Sam Fox Publishing Co (London) Ltd

BREAK DOWN AND LET IT ALL OUT

Words and Music by Van McCoy

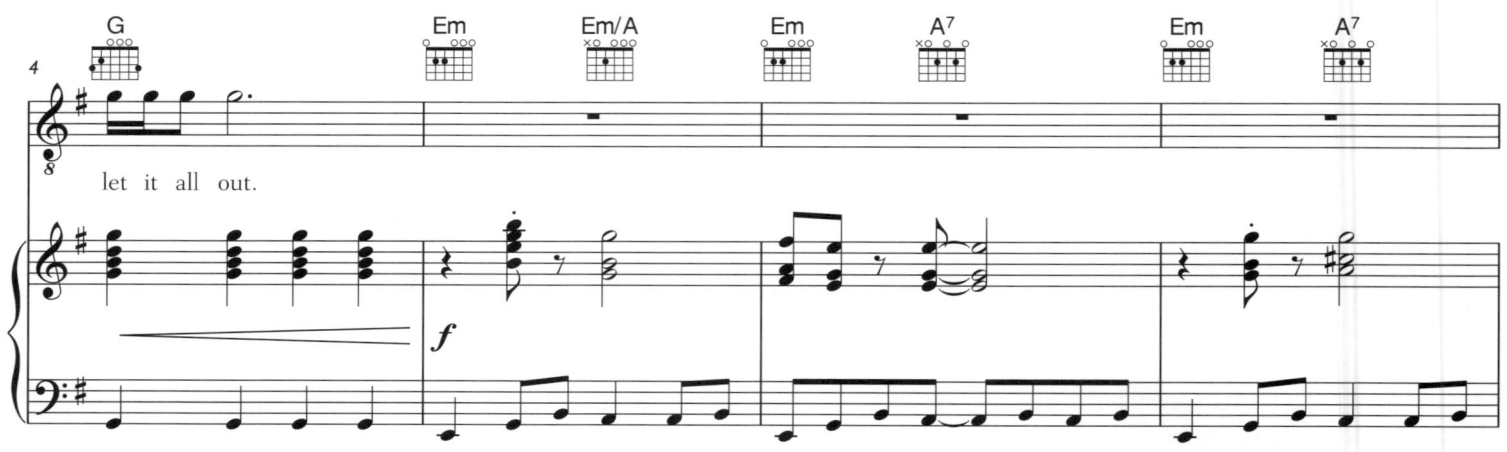
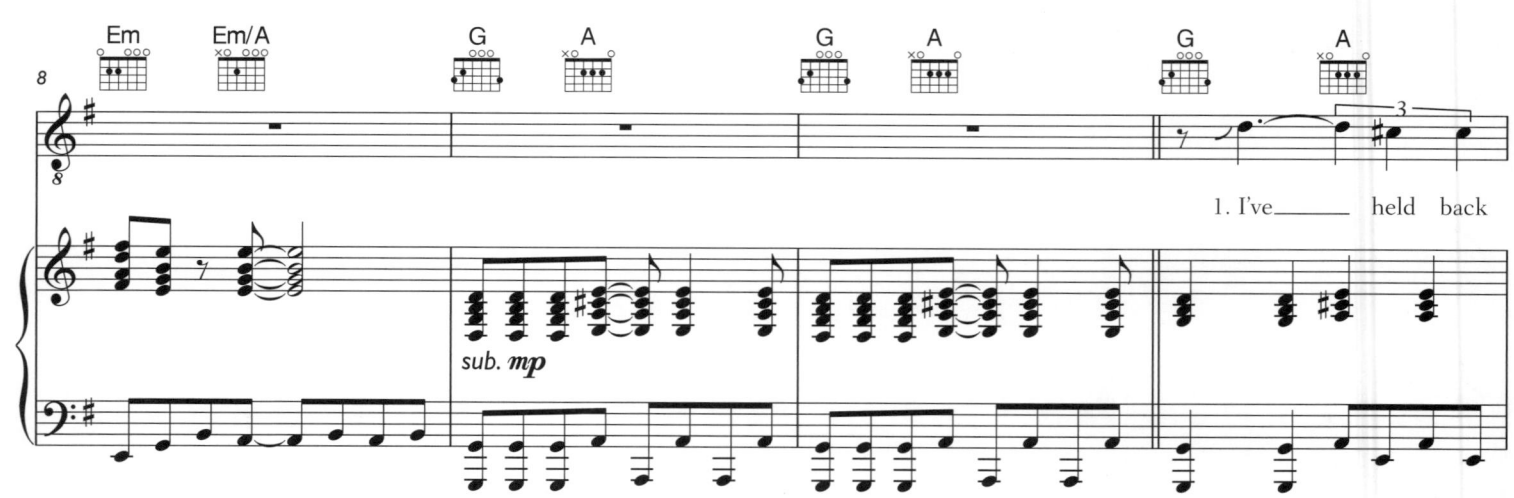

© 1965 EMI Blackwood Music Inc
EMI Songs Ltd

I GET ALONG WITHOUT YOU VERY WELL

Words by Hoagy Carmichael and George Terry
Music by Hoagy Carmichael

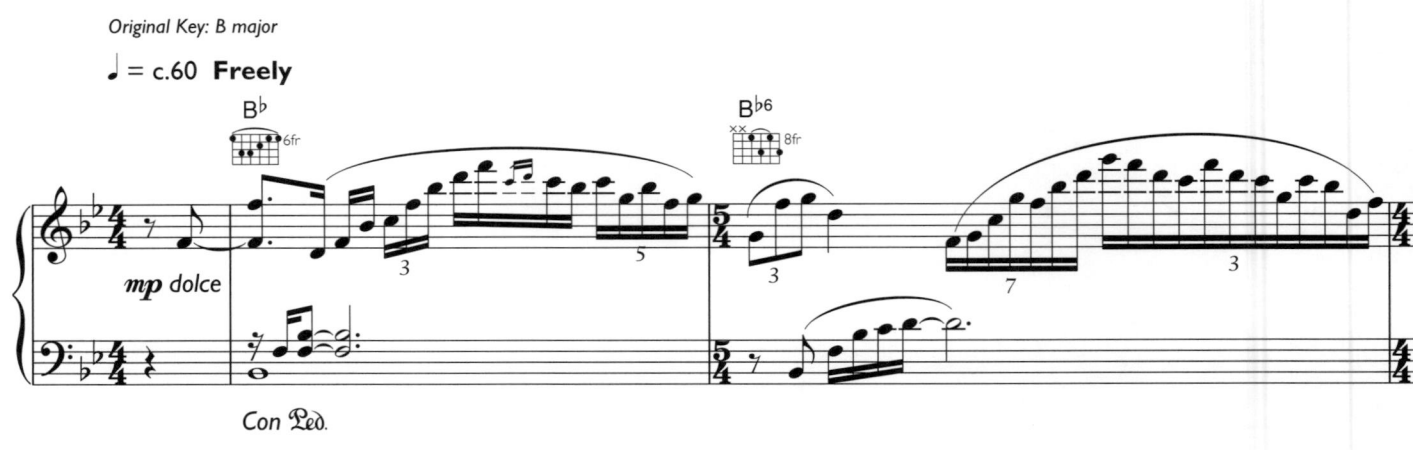

© 1939 Famous Music Corp
Peermusic (UK) Ltd

I SHALL BE RELEASED

Words and Music by Bob Dylan

© 1967 Dwarf Music (USA)
B Feldman & Co Ltd

I'M GONNA LEAVE YOU

Words and Music by Rudy Stevenson

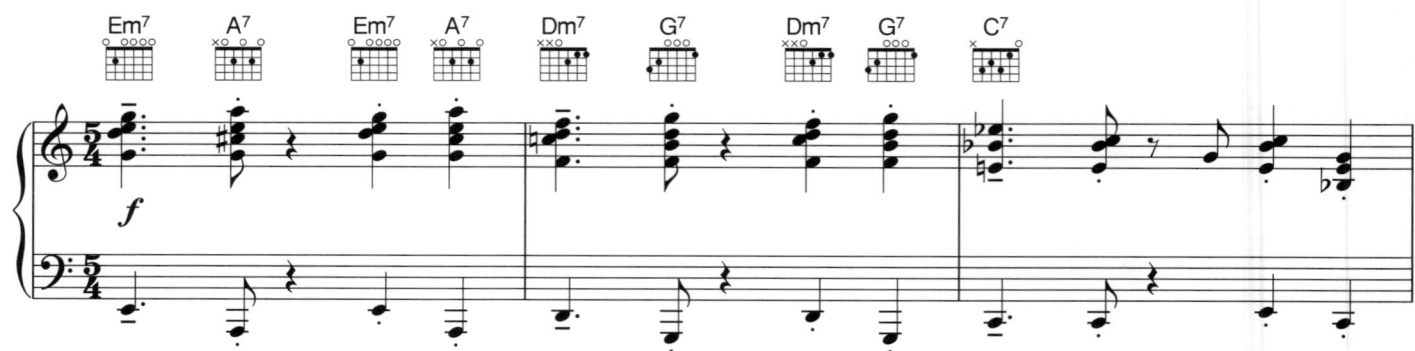
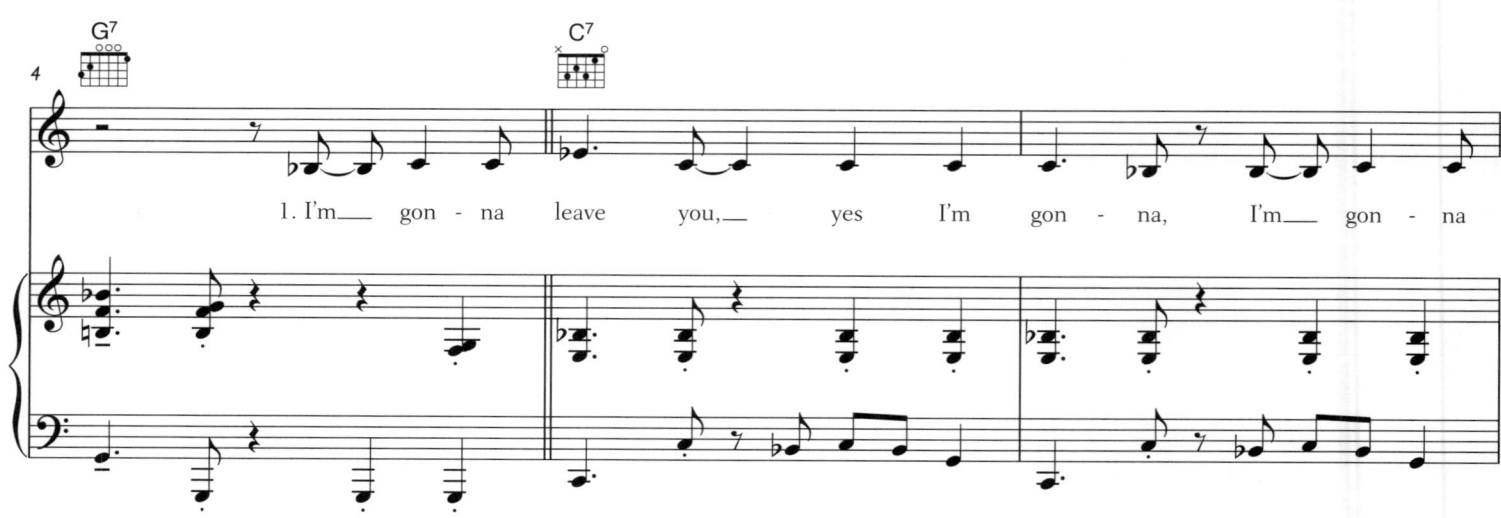

© 1967 Ninandy Music Co
EMI Tunes Ltd

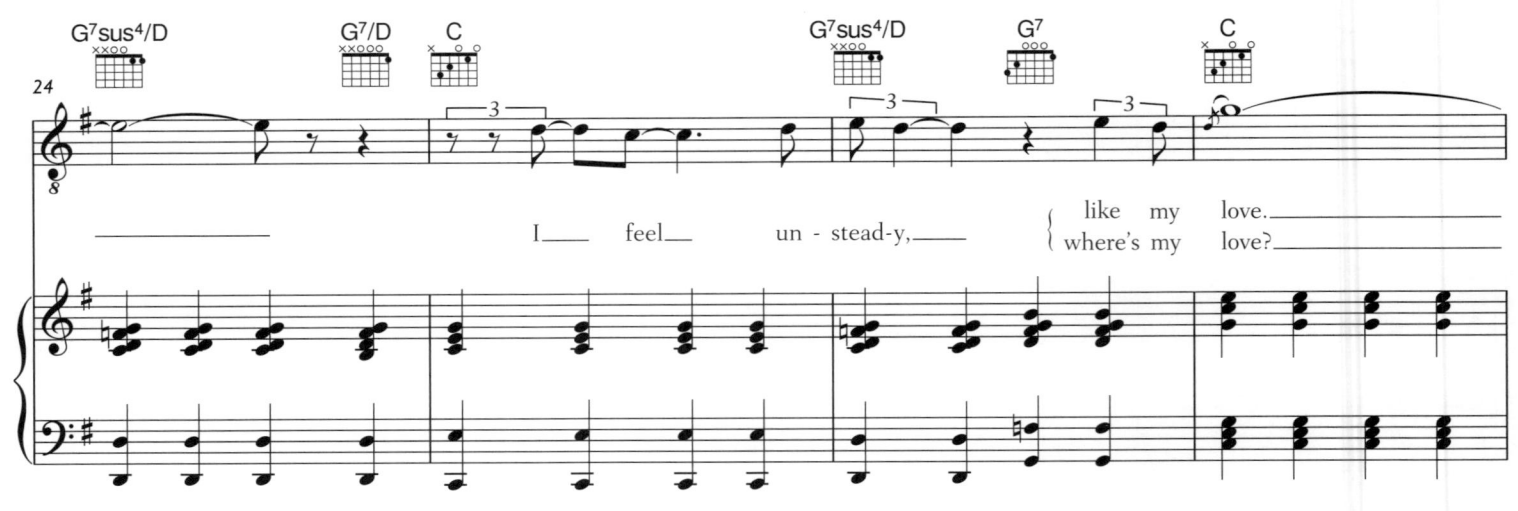
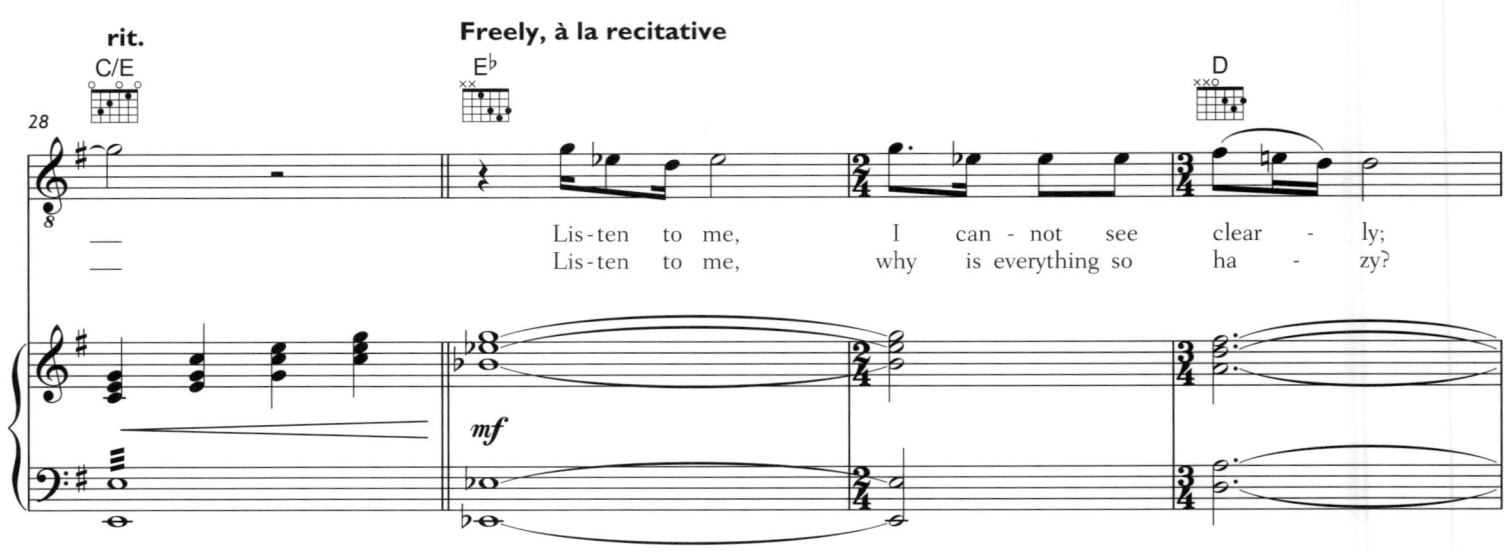
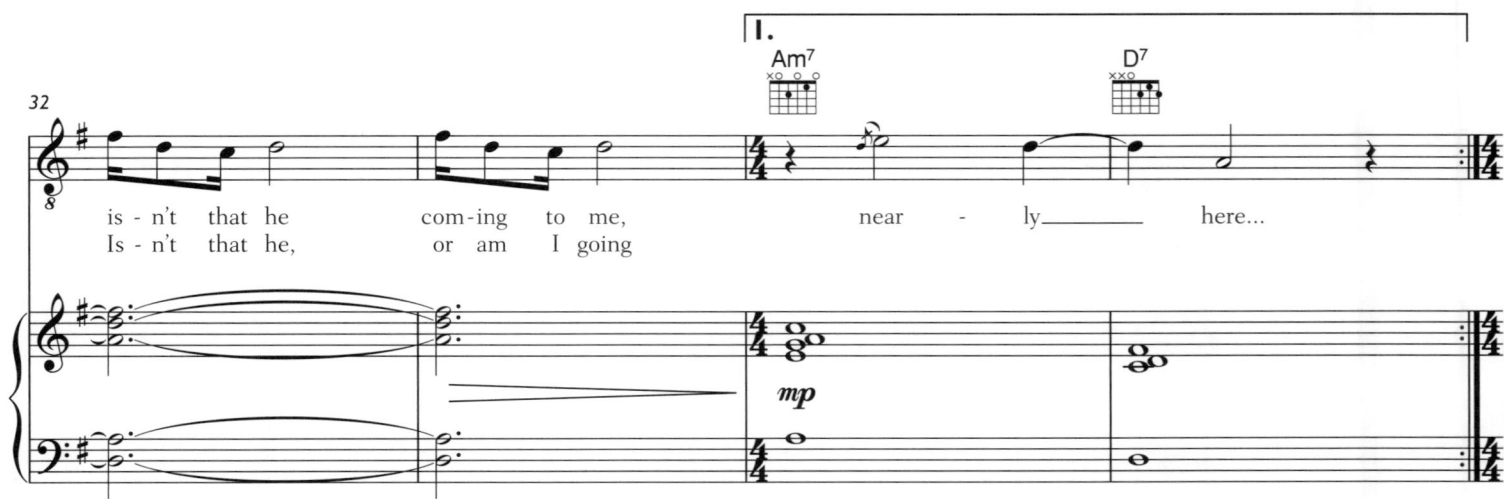

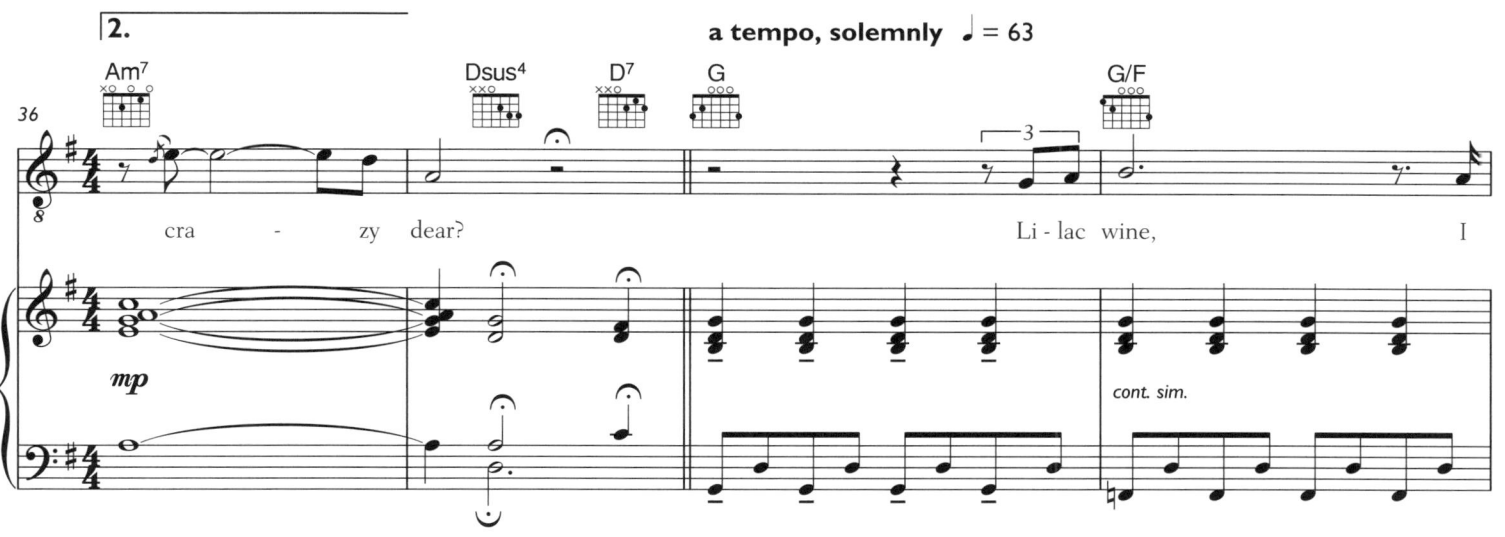

MY MAN'S GONE NOW

Words and Music by George Gershwin, Du Bose Heyward, Dorothy Heyward and Ira Gershwin

© 1935 Chappell & Co Inc
Warner/Chappell North America Ltd

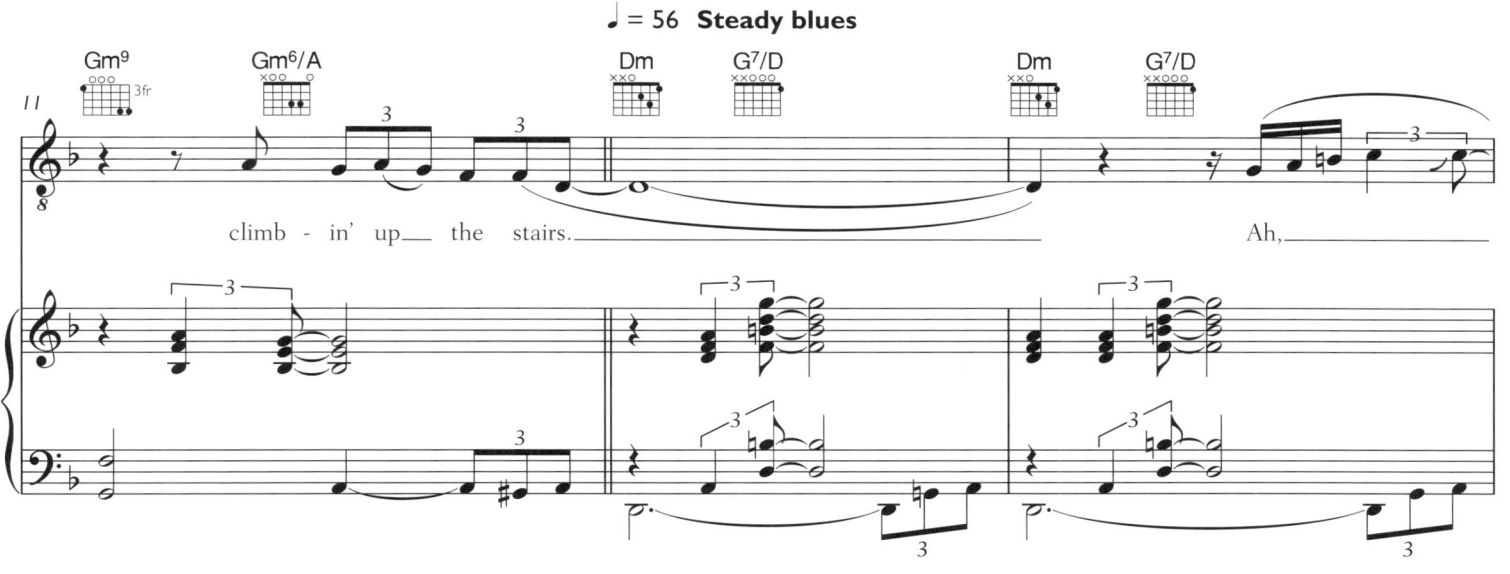
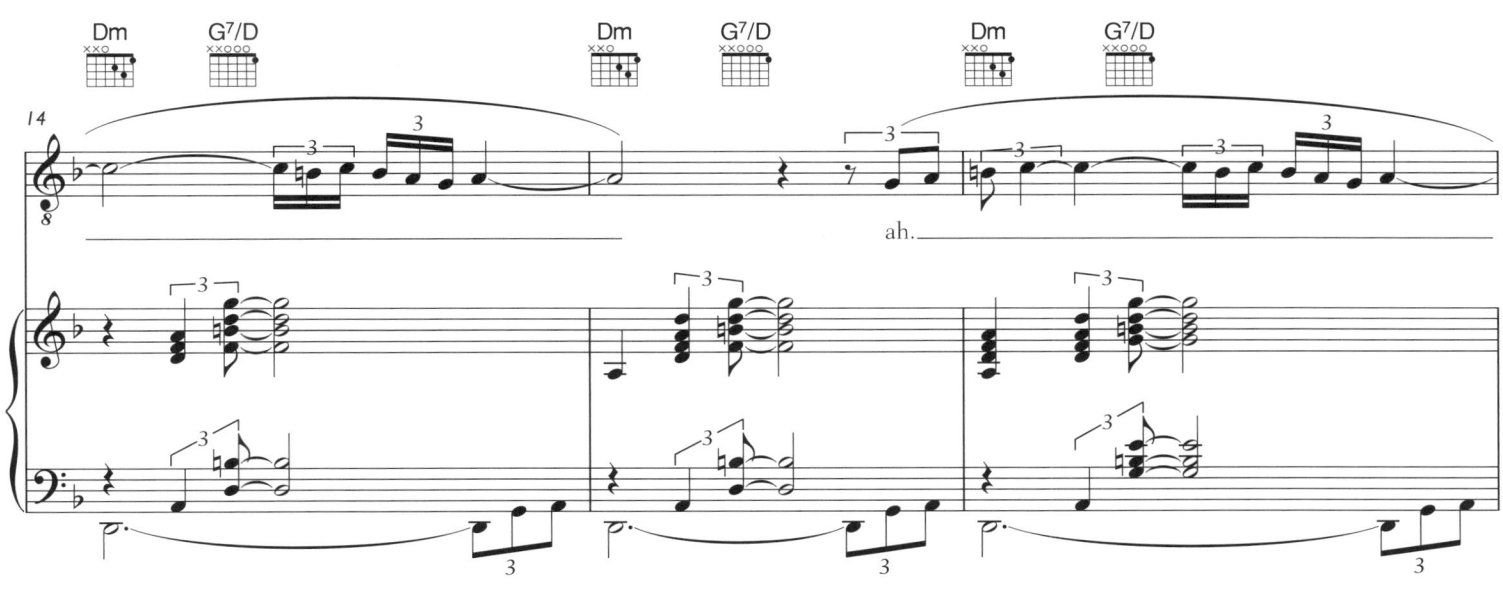
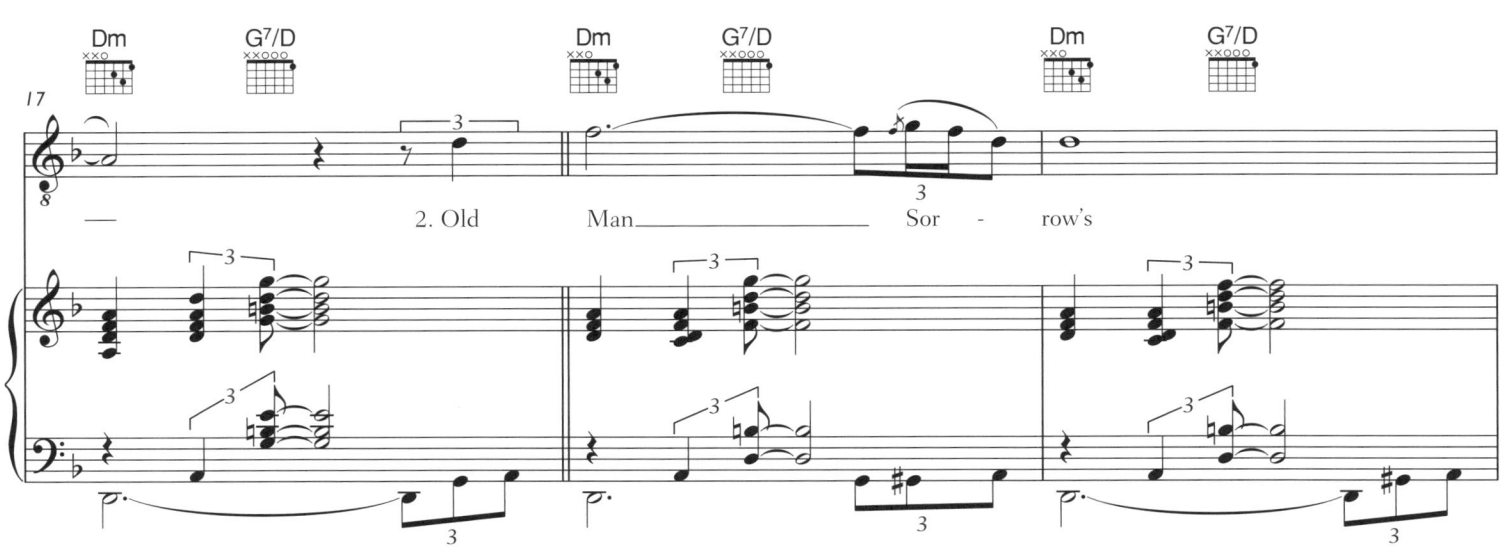

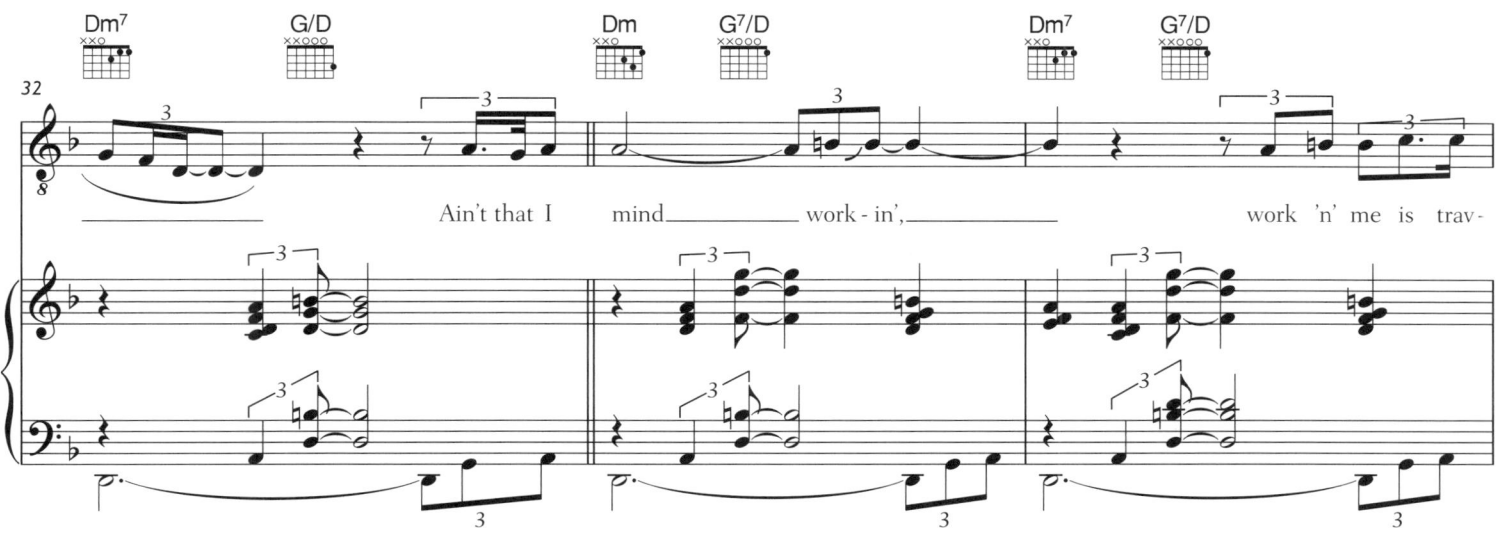
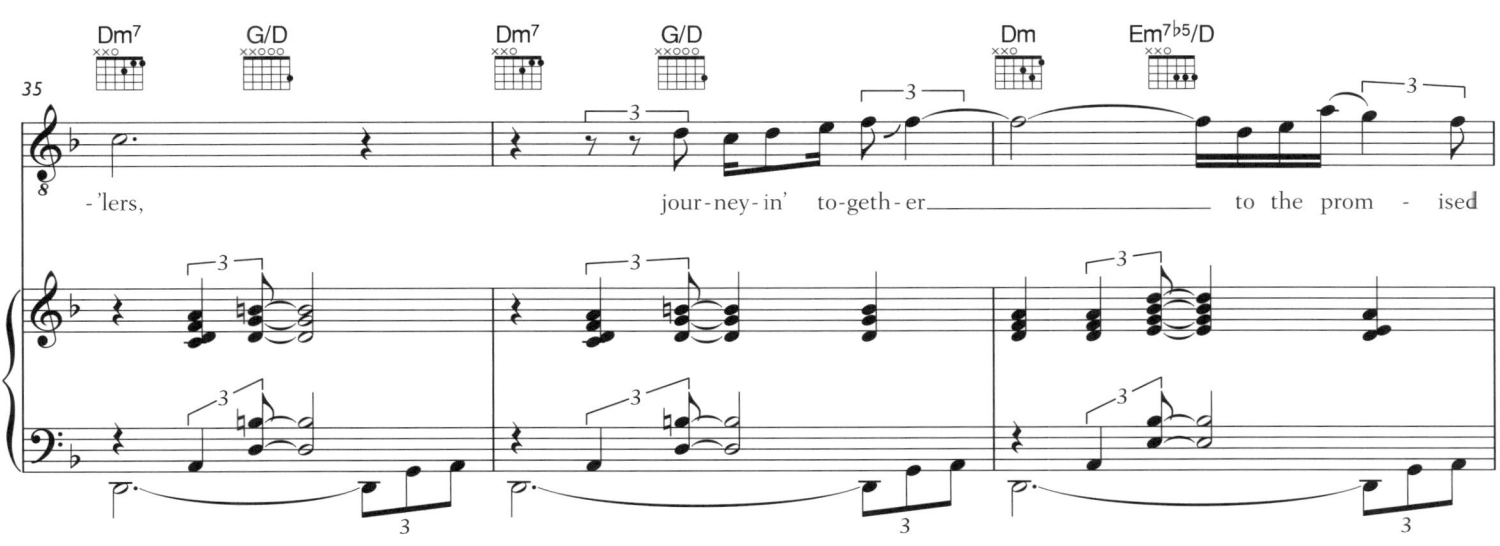
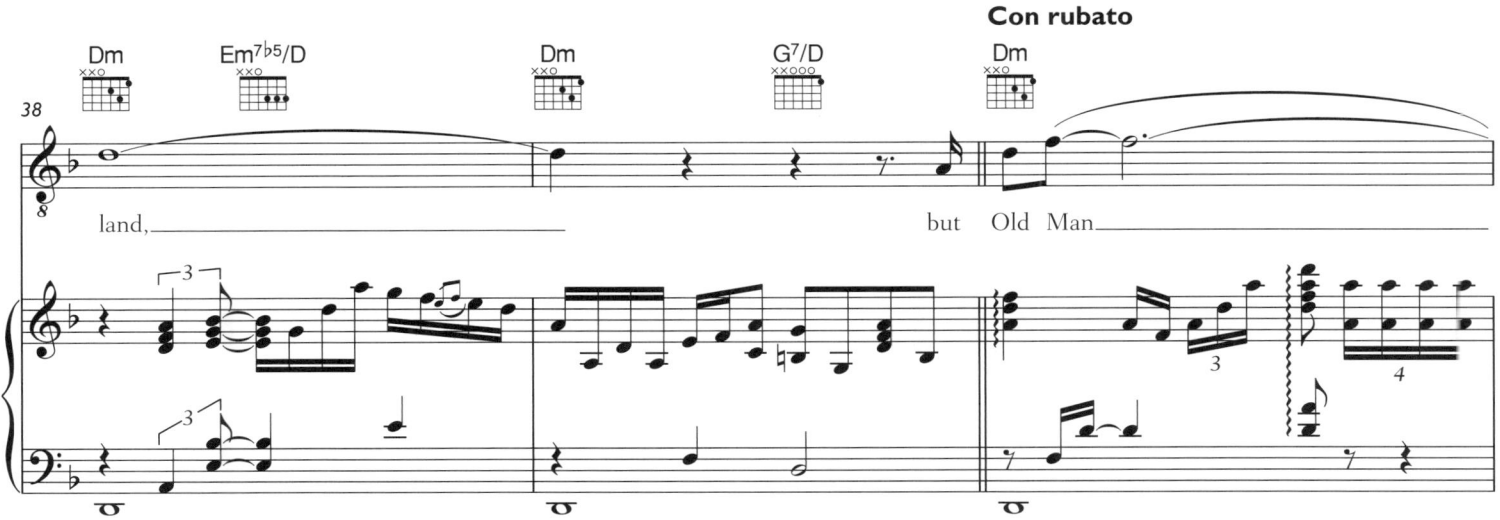

NEW WORLD COMING

Words and Music by Barry Mann and Cynthia Weil

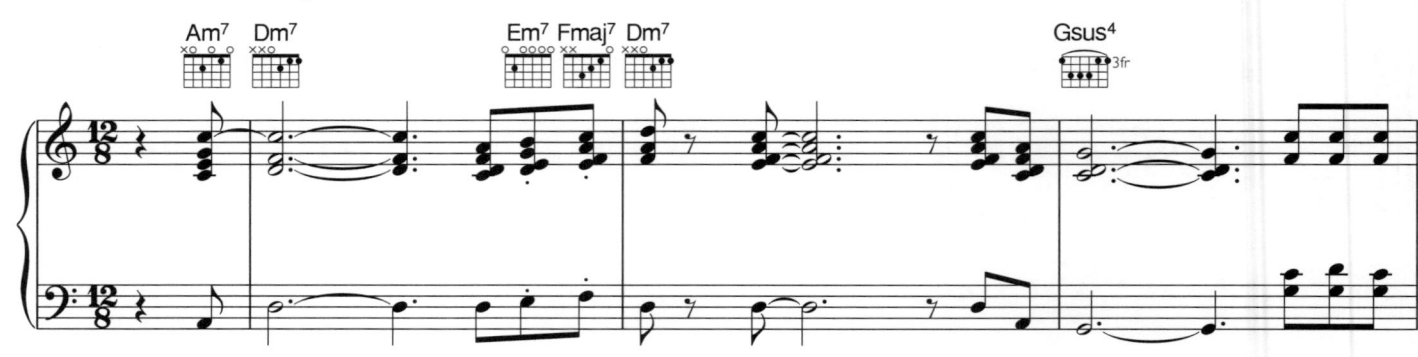
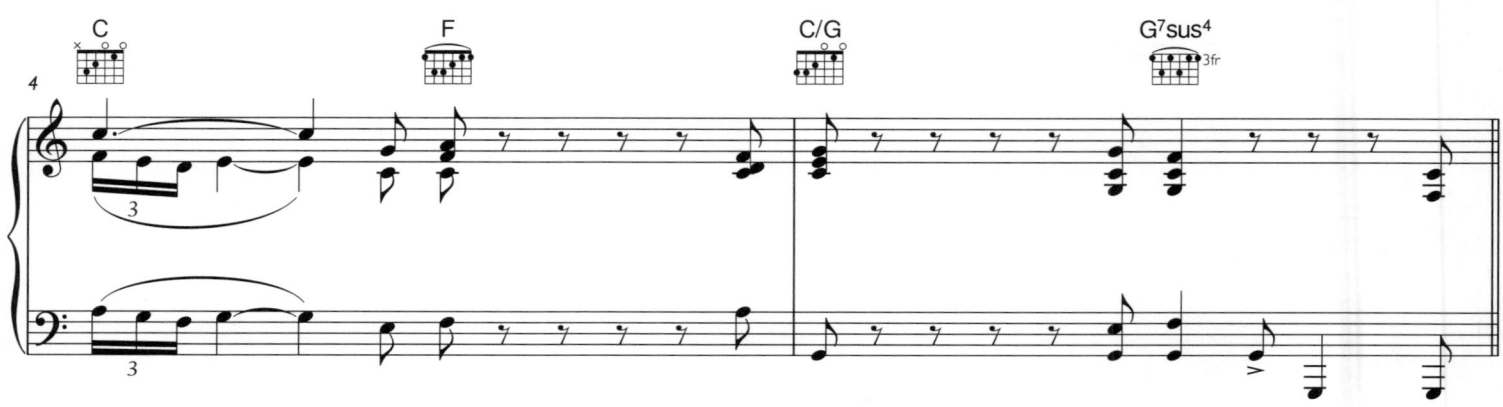

© 1969 Screen Gems-EMI Music Inc
Screen Gems-EMI Music Ltd

THE PUSHER

Words and Music by Hoyt Axton

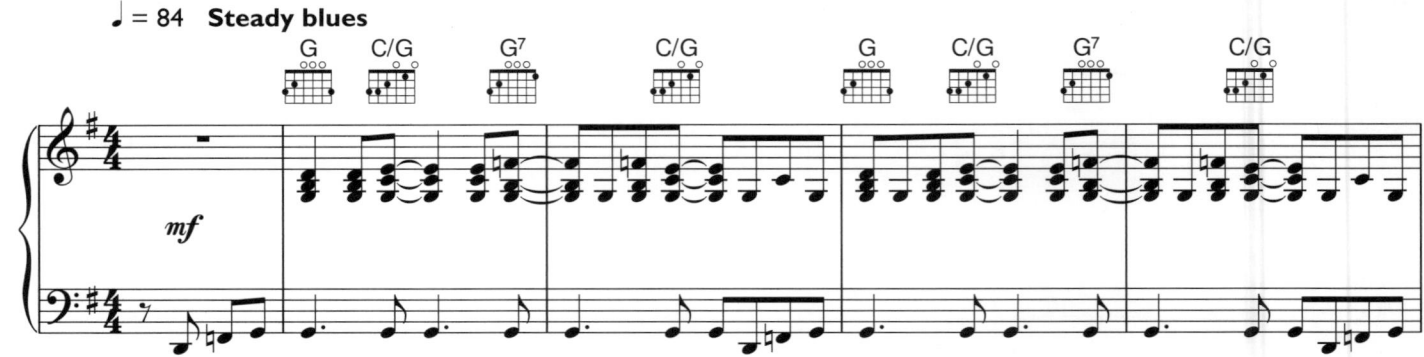
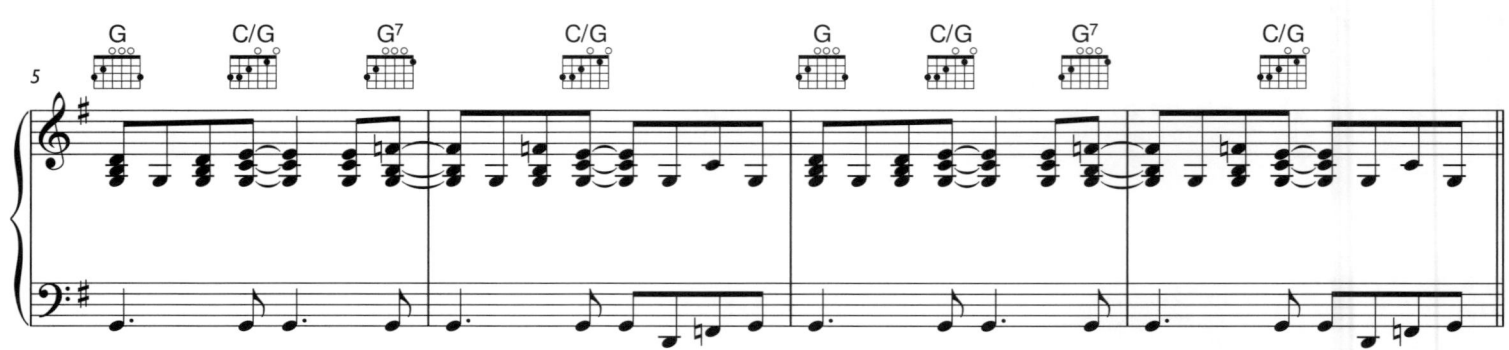

1. You know I smoked a lot of grass, oh Lord, and I popped a lot of

© 1967 Lady Jane Music
Universal Music Publishing Ltd

SEEMS I'M NEVER TIRED LOVIN' YOU

Words and Music by Cortez Franklin

© 1968 Ninandy Music Co and EMI Grove Park Music Inc
EMI Tunes Ltd

TURN ME ON

Words and Music by John D Loudermilk

♩. = 63 **Moderate Country**

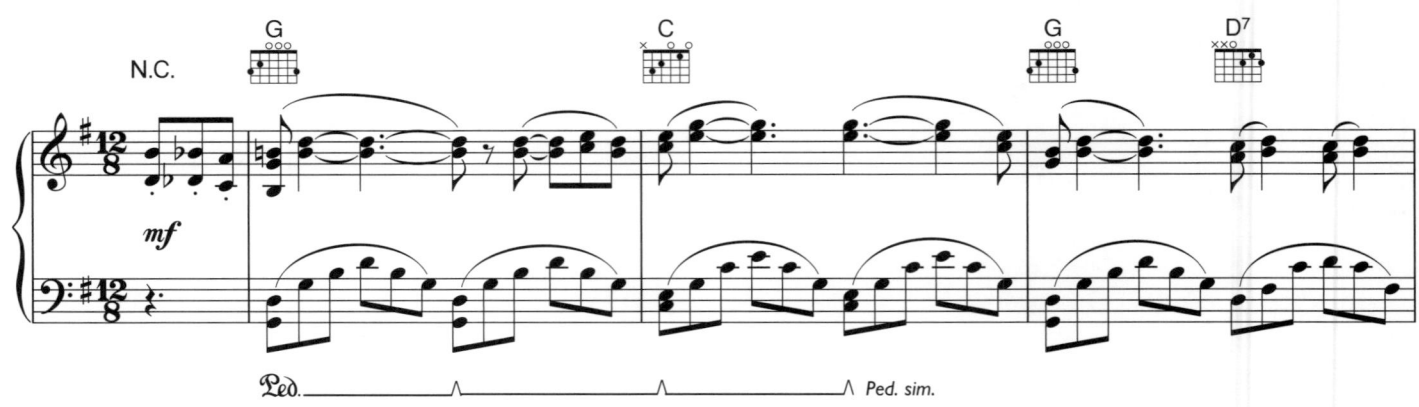
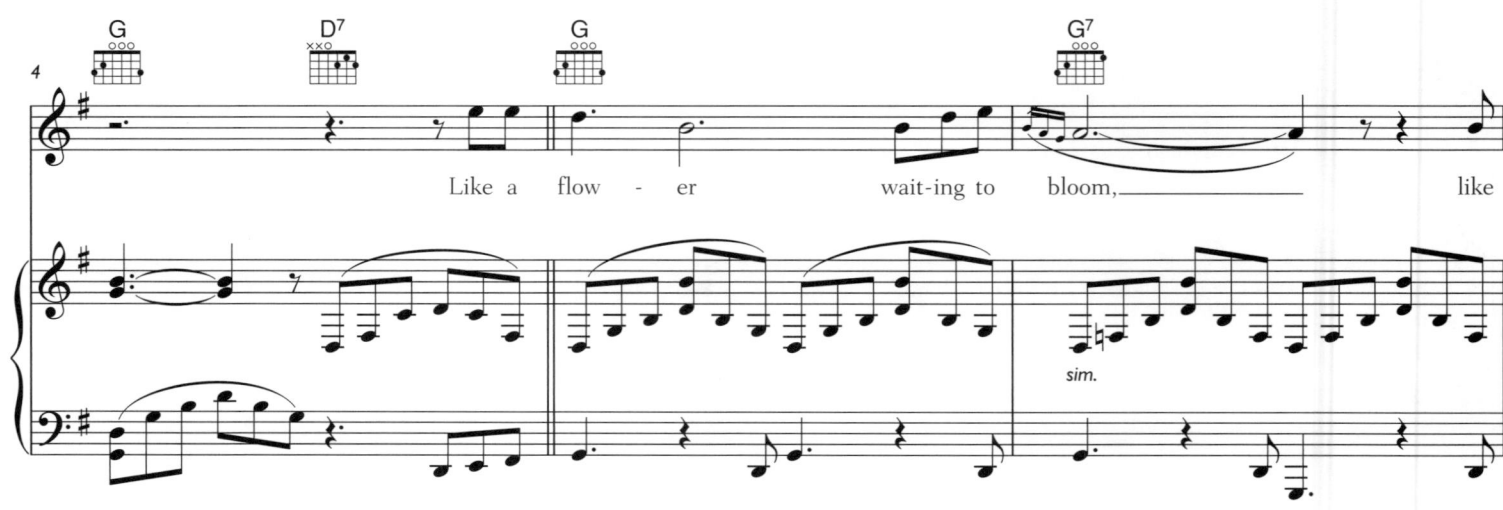

Like a flow-er wait-ing to bloom, like a light-bulb in a dark room, I'm here wait-ing for you to come

© 1967 Sony/ATV Acuff Rose Music
Sony/ATV Music Publishing (UK) Ltd

WILD IS THE WIND

Words by Ned Washington
Music by Dimitri Tiomkin

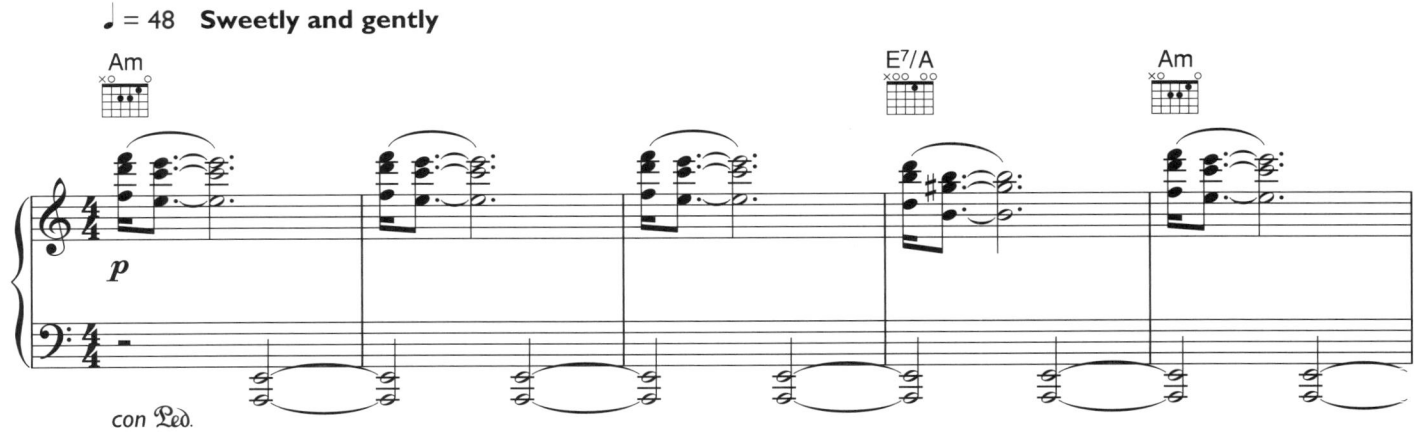
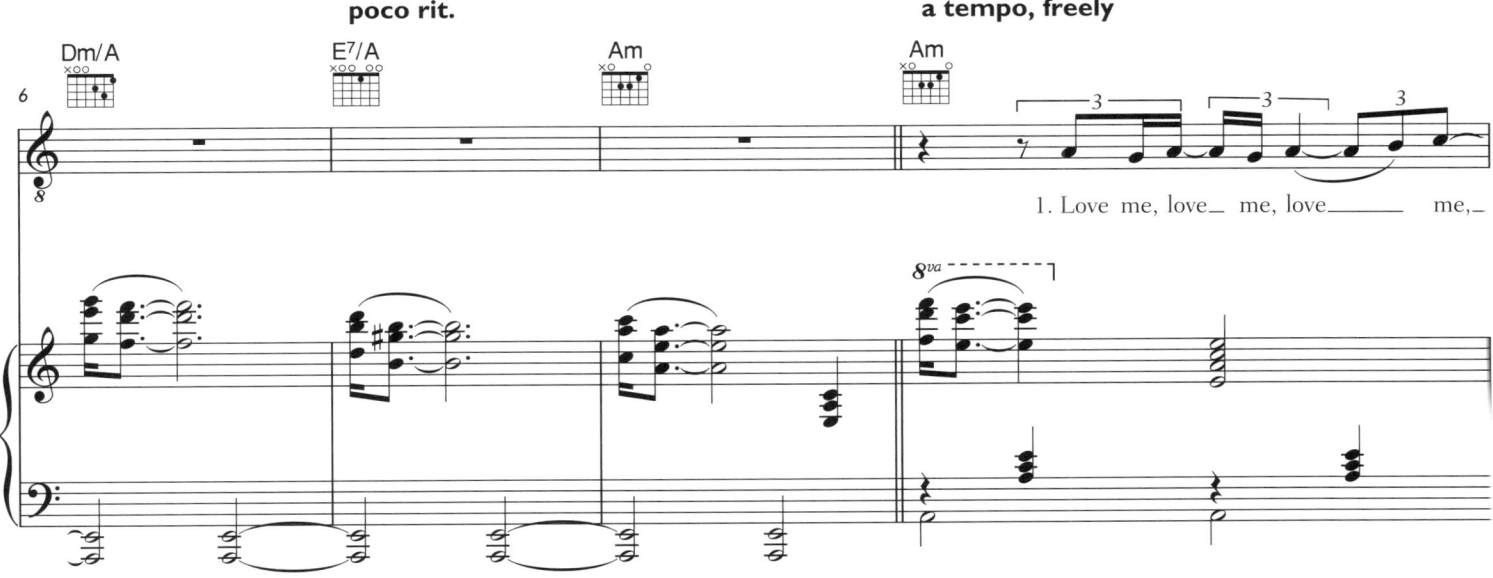
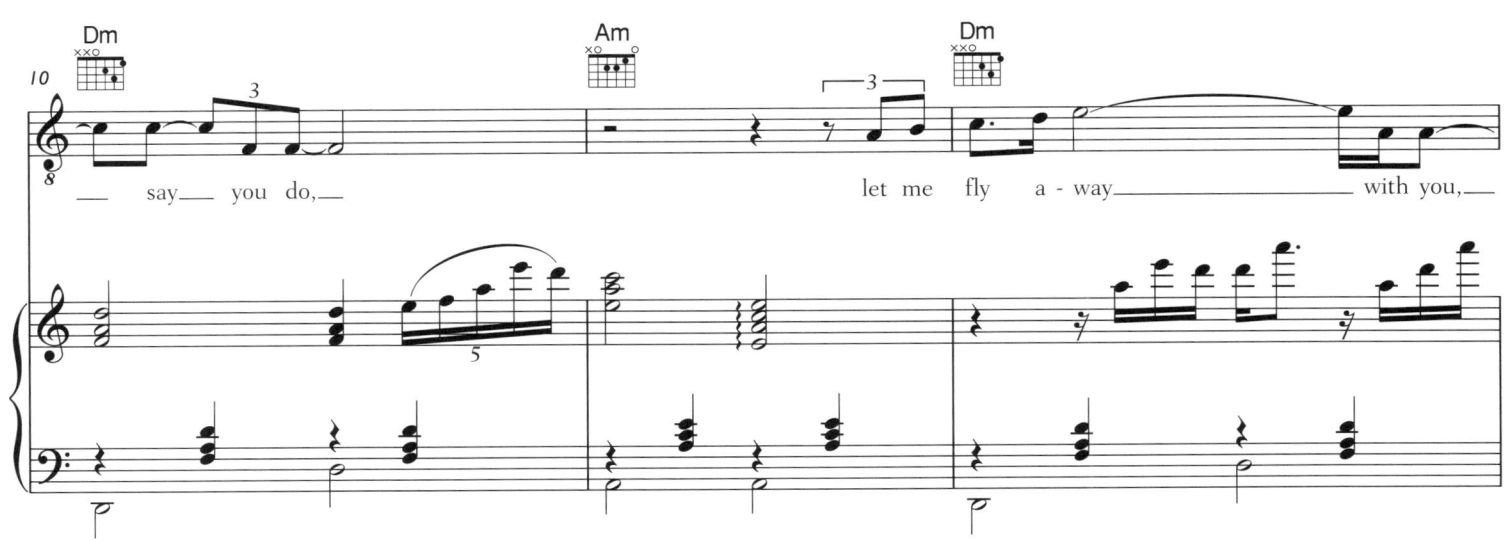

© 1957 Jungnickel-Ross Inc and Largo Music Inc
Carlin Music Corp and BMG Music Publishing Ltd

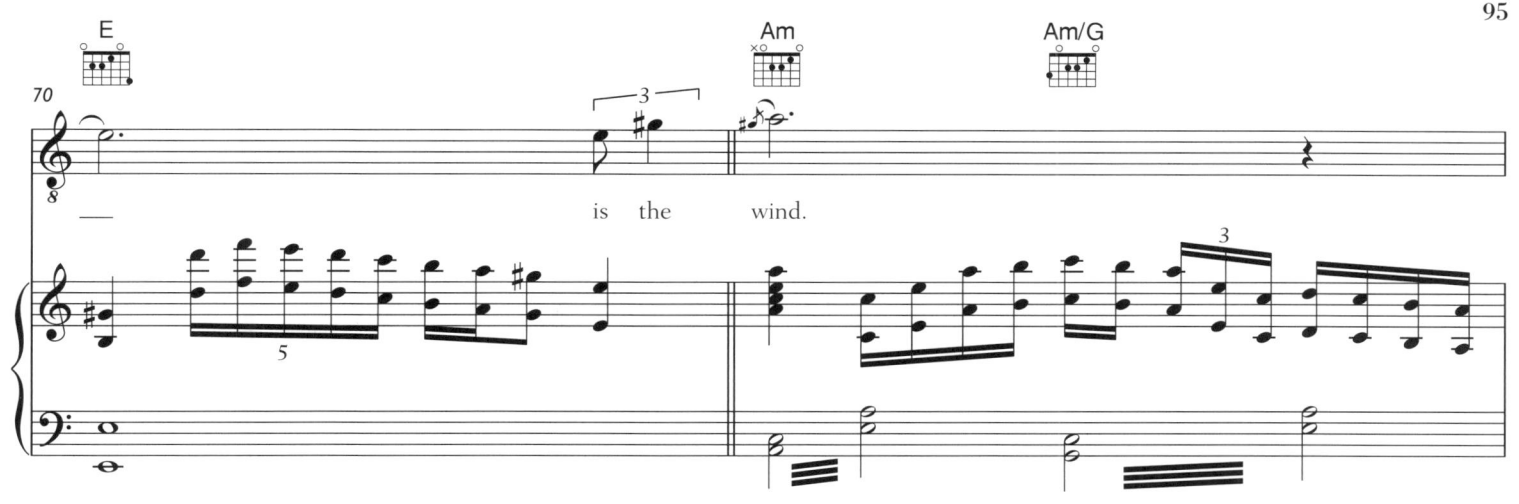
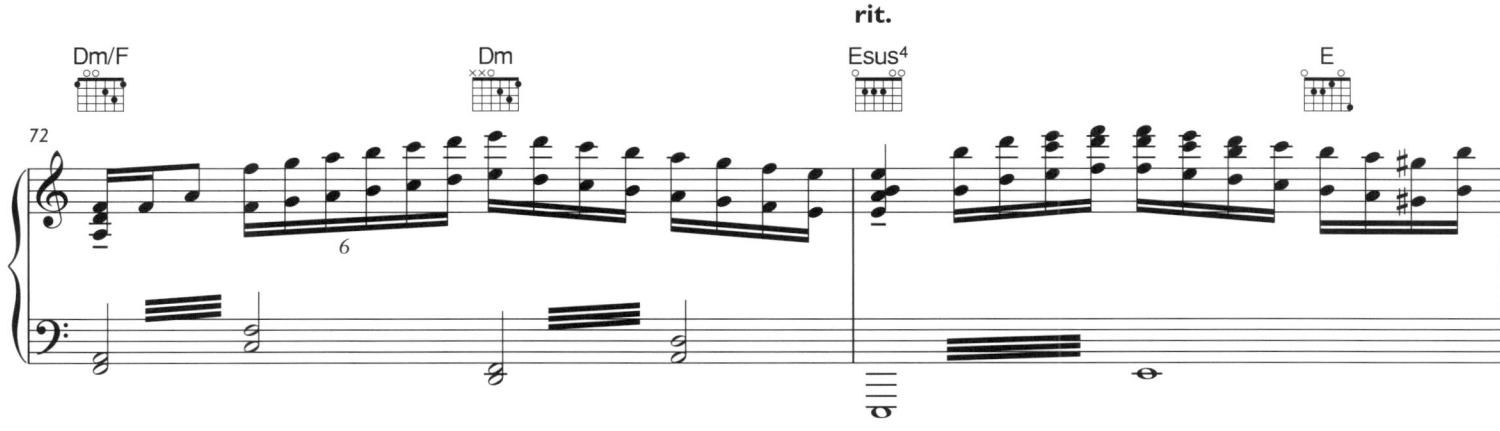

Nina Simone — The Piano Songbook

Nina Simone Piano Songbook Vol.1 (PVG)
ISBN: 0-571-52863-5

Ain't Got No, I Got Life
Don't Let Me Be Misunderstood
Feeling Good
I Loves You Porgy
I Put A Spell On You
I Think It's Going To Rain Today
I Want A Little Sugar In My Bowl
I Wish I Knew How It Would Feel To Be Free
The Look Of Love
Mr. Bojangles
My Baby Just Cares For Me
Nobody's Fault But Mine
Since I Fell For You
Sinnerman
To Be Young, Gifted and Black

To buy Faber Music publications or to find out about the full range of titles available
please contact your local music retailer or Faber Music sales enquiries:

Faber Music Ltd, Burnt Mill, Elizabeth Way, Harlow CM20 2HX
Tel: +44 (0) 1279 82 89 82   Fax: +44 (0) 1279 82 89 83
sales@fabermusic.com   fabermusicore.com